HINTS

ON

IRREGULAR CAVALRY,

ITS

CONFORMATION, MANAGEMENT AND USE IN BOTH A
MILITARY AND POLITICAL POINT OF VIEW.

BY

CAPT. CHARLES FARQUHAR TROWER,

MAJOR OF BRIGADE,

H. H. THE NIZAM'S CAVALRY.

CALCUTTA:

W. THACKER AND CO.—ST. ANDREW'S LIBRARY.

1845.

TO

LIEUT.-COL. JAMES BLAIR,

THE SENIOR OFFICER SERVING WITH IRREGULAR CAVALRY

IN INDIA,

THE FOLLOWING PAGES ARE INSCRIBED WITH

THE SINCEREST FEELINGS OF REGARD

AND ESTEEM, BY

C. F. TROWER.

CHAPTER I.

INTRODUCTION.

WE are taught in boyhood, and prove in after life, that in all dealing 'honesty is the best policy;' and I am inclined to think, following out that proverb, that the best excuse I can make for pubblishing the following pages, is, giving extracts from the correspondence which has led me into print.

MY DEAR C———,

After a search of many days amongst my ill-assorted papers, I think I have collected all the loose 'memoranda' regarding the subjects connected with irregular Cavalry, upon which you requested to be furnished with my 'opinions.' Such as they are, you are very welcome to them; and I hope, (I must confess the hope is faint,) that they will realize the very partial expectations you have formed of them. Your acuteness will

B

not fail to perceive that they have been noted down at various periods, and that a strong bias towards a race of people whom I greatly regard, and a service that I love, pervades the whole of them. This, on my part, is only natural. I have lived much amongst natives, and on such terms of intimacy with their nobles and gentles as few European officers strive to attain. I have long been attached to, and even before I joined, I saw much of, the Native Horse of India. In its ranks I reckon some of my best friends. I *know* that the material of which they are formed is not surpassed, even if equalled, by that of any branch of the Native Army of India: and of the gallant and loyal spirit which actuates them I am convinced, and my conviction is authorized by the proof which the conduct of the Irregular Cavalry of all the Presidencies has afforded in our late campaigns. I do not advance all this as an *excuse* for entertaining a good opinion of them. I do not deem an excuse necessary; but I merely mention it to *fortify* some ideas and suggestions which

I have brought forward, much canvassed even amongst those best capable of judging, and on the pros and cons of which even ' Doctors differ.' *******

The reply to this from my friend was as follows:—

" MY DEAR TROWER,—I am greatly obliged to you for the perusal of your notes. They contain a mass of interesting and valuable information, which I regret should be suffered to lie unknown and unheeded at the bottom of your well-worn camel-trunks at Amba. I wish I could persuade you to brush them up into shape, and launch them forth in print. I am not aware of the existence of any work which affords information regarding that very peculiar service, the Irregular Cavalry, or which would serve as a sort of manual to an officer when first appointed to Native Horse. The printed book of " Revised Rules and Regulations for the guidance of the Nizam's Army," which you sent me, certainly does not do so, though good as far as it goes: but it is about as likely that one should become a good General from reading the Mutiny Act and Hough's Case Book, as that the perusal of the aforesaid " Rules, &c." will serve to form an officer for Irregular Horse.

Consider this hint, and at your leisure work up these notes of yours, and I will bet the amount of the Lord Bishop's Abstract for one month against my pittance for ditto, that the pamphlet will be kindly received." * * * * * *

Now I should be sorry to go halves in my friend's stake, nor am I vain enough to believe that his partial opinion will be concurred in by others, not biassed by feelings of friendship: but as I do hope that the following pages may be of some use, I have followed his advice and ' brushed up' my notes 'into some shape,' and herewith launch them forth.

The Irregular Horse have been much increased of late, and form now a very large portion of our Indian Cavalry. They deserve, if only from their numbers, some notice; and their organization, and the best system to be pursued regarding them, should be more generally known.　I humbly submit my ideas upon these important points.　If the following pages tend to have this effect, if what I have advanced, leads to a more careful selection of those who are sent to serve with and command them, if it remove certain common but very erroneous impressions regarding a good and gallant body of men, if it cause in the slightest degree a more just appreciation of the Native Horsemen of India, I shall be fully and completely satisfied.

CHAPTER II.

———

Selection of European Officers—Qualifications
necessary—Opinion of the late Captain G.
Sydenham and Mr. H. Russell—Local Officers
—Advantages possessed by them in the Nizam's
Army—Objections to employment of them in com-
mand—Promotion by merit not seniority.

———

BEFORE proceeding with the subject I have
proposed to myself, I would wish to make some
observations regarding the selection of European
Officers for service with Irregular Cavalry.

It is, I imagine, universally admitted, that the
efficiency of native soldiers generally depends on
their European Officers. If this is true with
reference to Regular Corps, with their compara-
tively full complement of Officers, how much more
need is there of peculiar qualifications in an Officer
sent to a Regiment to which but *three* Europeans
are attached.

Of the description of men who compose our Irregular Cavalry, I shall treat hereafter, but I may here remark, that they are a class who are peculiarly led and influenced by their respect and affection for, and their admiration of the soldier-like and manly qualities of their superiors.

The selection of an European Officer to serve with Irregular Cavalry, instead therefore, of being a mere matter of interest should be made with much circumspection. His standing in the Company's Army is of no importance so long as he possesses the requisite qualifications, which may thus be briefly enumerated. He should have a *very considerable* knowledge of Hindoostanee, more especially a colloquial knowledge, so as to be able to converse *really fluently* with those entrusted to him —not that bastard degree of acquirement contemplated by the Governor-General in G. O. of the 20th of April, 1844—he should be well versed in their customs, habits, and peculiar modes of thinking and feeling, which can alone be acquired by mixing much with natives. He should be a man of admirable temper, never hasty, firm, yet patient; for many things apparently trifling to our ideas, are of much importance in their estimation: and it is a great (although a frequent) mistake to judge of the conduct of natives by the standard which we have set up for our own. Physically he should be strong and of good constitution, of active habits of mind and body, and an excellent horseman. He should be one likely to excel in athletic exercises or feats of horsemanship; for, as with all demi-barbarians these physical advantages are held in high estimation by the class of men composing Irregular Cavalry, and the mixing with the men in their warlike sports creates affection, as the excelling them in their own line produces admiration. He should be of easy access, ever ready to hear each man's complaint. He should be a man of good nerves, and of a considerable spirit of enterprize; generally intelligent and sensible; for he is often placed in circumstances which call for the exercise of tact and great judgment.

⋅ Let me add to the above the following opinions of two as able judges on this subject as the ranks of our Indian Statesmen have produced.

" On the other hand British officers should uniformly observe a conciliatory demeanour towards the Commanders, and should, therefore, be men who had maintained frequent intercourse with natives, and who were acquainted with their language and habits, besides possessing that spirit of enterprize and strength of constitution so requisite in a service of great uncertainty and fatigue."*

Alluding to the sort of officers required with Irregular Cavalry Mr. H. Russell thus writes : " He would have to lead and direct them on all occasions, to guide them by his knowledge, and encourage them by his example; and above all he would have the difficult task of surmounting the prejudices of caste and religion, and reconciling the men to act with cheerfulness under his authority.   But for this duty, difficult and com-

* Capt. George Sydenham to H. Russell, Esquire, 1st April 1816.

c

plicated as it is, I have no hesitation in
recommending Captain Davis. *   *   *   *
The integrity of his character, his known gal-
lantry and enterprize, his temper and experience,
his habits of personal activity, his acquaintance
with the language, manners, and prejudices of
the natives, his dexterity in the use of all their
weapons, and his skill in their peculiar modes
of Horsemanship, eminently qualify him for such
a charge."

15th April, 1816.

To the Secy. to Govt. Fort William.

The great rock against which so many officers
when sent into Irregular Corps make shipwreck,
is the belief, that by the introduction of such and
such new measures, they can make their men
more nearly approximate to the Regular Cavalry.
Now no man of ordinary sense should for an
instant attempt to make any sort of com-
parison between Regular and Irregular Cavalry.
There is no greater resemblance between them
than between Macedon and Monmouth. " Look

you there is salmons in both," but it goes no
further. The duties that might probably be required from each on service would be entirely different. There is nothing so distasteful to the majority
of natives as change of any sort, above all any
change affecting their purse or their prejudices:
and the death of Colonel Davis, who was murdered
by his own troops, is a melancholy proof of this. I
would give a piece of advice to all officers enter-
ing Irregular Cavalry in the words of a vulgar
proverb, "Do not try to make a silken purse out
of a sow's ear." The Irregular Horse, when kept
as such, are excellent troops, admirably adapted for
the duties to be expected from them; but you will
not make 'Horse Guards' of them; and every
attempt towards this Sisyphian task will only roll
back on yourself and impair the efficiency you
have at present. It is the dislike, the dread of
our system of European discipline which prevents
many of the more respectable portion of the warlike classes of India from enlisting in the ranks of
our Regular Army. This crushes the spirit of the

native—it is uncalled for, and in his case perfectly unnecessary. With the more active-minded European soldier leisure is generally only another term for license :—he must he doing something ; and if he has not his duties to attend to, the chances are that he is in some mischief. The reverse is the case with the more indolent Asiatic,—leisure to him is luxury: and when relieved from his work, you will generally find him ruminating over his hookah, or placidly attending to his domestic concerns. I have known more harm done by silly alterations and changes regarding dress or accoutrements, or in the petty details of the interior economy of a troop, introduced with the best intention by some injudicious European officer, than those not conversant with the peculiar temper of Native Horsemen would conceive possible to arise from such causes.

To the Irregular Cavalry of His Highness the Nizam, as well as to some of the Hindostan Irregular Corps, Local Officers are attached, and amongst them there have been, and no doubt are as good and efficient officers as any ever furnished from the Royal or Company's Army; but in the Nizam's Service, they have privileges granted to them which much militate against the interests and just claims of other Officers. By a late regulation they are permitted a furlough to Europe for three years, either on sick certificate or private affairs, with the power of returning to the command or Staff situation they may have held on departure from India. This has put an almost entire check upon promotion and the chances of succeeding to the Staff situations of that Army; and as the Eastern proverb hath it, ' When hope dies, emulation and zeal languish.' It is an advantage not enjoyed by officers on the Staff of the Honorable Company's Army: and either the officers of the latter service, attached to that of the Nizam should be permitted a like indulgence, or this regulation should be much modified.

But there is one very serious objection to the employment of Local officers in situations of command; an objection that may be severely felt on any occasion, when the troops of a Contingent Force may be called upon to act on service with detachments of Her Majesty's or the Honorable Company's Army. Let us suppose a case of a Local Brigadier or Commandant, an old and intelligent officer, to whom some particular duty is entrusted, and in the execution of which the aid of any branch of the Company's or Her Majesty's troops was called in; if this detachment was but a section under command of the youngest Ensign, he would immediately, in virtue of his commission, supercede the Local officer, who would have to act under his orders; and most serious detriment to the public service might arise therefrom, or what is more likely to happen some Company's officer immediately under his orders would at once assume command on being joined by such detachment. I am not supposing an impossible case. Many have happened where the forces of the Nizam and the Company have acted together: two very recently; at Baloorghee.

in 1840, where both Artillery and Infantry were
called on to aid the Irregular Cavalry of the
Nizam; and at Balapore in 1843; but on both
those occasions the officer commanding was
fortunately a Company's officer. This and other
reasons not requisite to be detailed in this place,
would seem to render it unadvisable to promote
Local Officers to the higher commands, unless it
would suit the views of Government to furnish
them with Local commissions from itself. There
would be no breach of engagement in thus treating
them, as I believe, most of the Local Officers, on
receiving their first appointment as Local Lieute-
nants, were tacitly given to understand that they
would not rise to commands; as indeed is the
rule with Local Officers attached to Irregular Corps
of the Bengal Presidency with one exception in
favor of Major Forster. The recent case of Capt.
James Skinner is in point. From his being a
Local officer he was not permitted to succeed to
the command of his father's Regiment; a succession, which from peculiar circumstances connected

with Colonel Skinner and his services, was expected as hereditary.

The most strict and full reports of the qualifications in every respect of officers attached to Irregular Cavalry should be called for and *acted upon,* otherwise the confidential reports of commanding officers are rendered but a farce; and in a service of this nature, seniority should never. be considered to give a claim for promotion except in those rare cases where merit may be equal. If the system of promotion according to merit is advisable anywhere, surely it must be more particularly so in a service where so much, indeed I may say *all,* depends upon the qualifications of the European officer. In acting strictly upon this rule also in the Nizam's Army, no promises that I am aware of would be .violated, for none giving promotion by seniority have been made.. On the contrary it has been frequently the practice of late years to introduce officers into the service, who have superseded many already attached to it.

I cannot conclude these observations without remarking how greatly better the selection of officers for the Irregular Cavalry of the Nizam's Army was, when patronage was entrusted to the Resident at Hyderabad for the time being. All patronage may be abused, but it is just as probable that the Governor-General or the Governor of any of the minor Presidencies should be influenced by partiality as the Resident of Hyderabad; all being equally supposed to be gentlemen of integrity. The chances in favor of the Resident making a better selection are, that, being on the spot, he is better able than the Governor-General to form an opinion of the qualifications requisite for the peculiar appointment he has to bestow; and in those cases where the situations, or promotions, go in the service, he has a much better knowledge of the character and claims of the various applicants.*

* Colonel Davis, Captains Pedlar, John and Eric Sutherland, H. Inglis, Byam, &c. were all selections made by the Resident at Hyderabad.

D

CHAPTER III.

*Silladars—their rights, character, and contract made
by them. The selection of Bargheers to be left
to them. Large Pagahs—the advantage of—and
in a political point of view. Irregular Cavalry
how rendered independent of the Commissariat.*

THE peculiar distinction of Irregular Cavalry
is that they are Sillidaree Horse; that is, in one
sense of the term, horses of this description of
force are not the property of the Government (as
in our corps of Regular Cavalry), but belong
either to their rider, or some other party who
contracts with the Government for a settled sum
to keep up a horse or a certain number of horses.
When the owner rides his own horse, or has
others belonging to him in the corps, he is termed
in the Deccan a Sillidar, or in Hindustan, a
"Khood-uspa." In the Irregular Cavalry of Hindostan, I believe that there are no Sillidars but

such as serve in person in the Corps; but in the
Poonah Auxiliary Horse, the Kurnool Horse, and
in the Cavalry of the Nizam there are many
" Be-noka" Sillidars. Officers of great experience and acknowledged judgment, have differed
much as to the propriety of allowing parties not
serving in person to become Sillidars, or the
owners of horses in our corps; and much has been
advanced on both sides of the question. Those
who object to the system of " Be-noka Sillidars"
(i. e. Sillidars not in the service) argue also that
the system of large Pagahs* is injurious, and that
the efficiency of Corps of Irregular Cavalry would
be improved were every man to become a Khood-
uspa or Sillidar riding his own horse and possessing no others. As the Sillidar class is certainly
the most important and most respectable in
the Irregular Cavalry, I shall enter somewhat in
detail into this question which affects the very
constitution of Native Horse. In doing so, I

* Pagah is here used to denote a considerable number of horses
—10, 50, 100 or more,—belonging to one Sillidar.

may here premise, that in my observations I allude, except where otherwise expressly stated, to the Nizam's Cavalry, as being the service with which I am personally best acquainted.

To discuss this question fairly it is necessary to call to mind the terms upon which many of the horsemen of India have been transferred to us from native states,—what agreements were entered into with the parties so transferred,—and how the Sillidar first acquired his right. The greater part of the present Nizam's Cavalry originally formed a portion of what was termed the Berar Horse. They were of two descriptions, Sirkaree and Jagheerdaree. The latter consisted chiefly of the large parties of Shums-ool-omra and Raja Rao Rumbah; but in consequence of the high rank of these chieftains they were not reduced to obedience to the local Government of Berar, and, indeed were scarcely under the control of the minister himself at Hyderabad. The rest were chiefly employed in the jagheers of their respective chieftains, and were not considered fit for the

public service. From these therefore no tranfers
were made to the Reformed Horse. But there
was a body of Jagheer Horse attached to Sulabut
Khan, which, from the regularity of its payment
and the admirable arrangement introduced by
·that chief, was considered little, if at all, inferior
.to the Sirkaree Cavalry. From this party the
·present 5th Regiment of the Nizam's Cavalry
·was formed.

The Sirkaree Cavalry was divided into several
Sheristas as they were called, or large bodies under
different Sheristadars or superintendents, to whom
the Government entrusted the payment and interior economy of their respective parties. " The
whole of the Sirkaree Cavalry are on the Sillidar
establishment as far as the Government are con-
·cerned ; but Commanders have the option of
entertaining Bargheers, and they in general
muster an equal number of horse of each description," is the testimony of Captain Sydenham,
who originally reformed the Nizam's Cavalry. In
1816 when this body of Cavalry was reformed,

and British Officers were attached, who superceded the Sheristadars, the troops were guaranteed the continuance of their long-established usages and customs. In the preceding quotation, I have shewn, that, as far as the Government were concerned (and we now stand in the place of that Government virtually) the Sillidar establishment prevailed. That establishment then, among others, was guaranteed. The Sillidar ' assamee'. or ' situation' has been long looked upon in the Irregular Cavalry of the Deccan as a ' property ;' as much so almost as the 'Potailee' or hereditary succession to the head authority of a village. This ' assamee' was not only permitted to be sold, but was allowed to be bequeathed from father to son, or for the subsistence of the widow or family of the Sillidar: and the sale or bequeathment was, in almost all cases, held valid. This power naturally rendered the situations or assamees valuable; and even at the present day in all native states a very considerable nuzzurana is given for the permission to keep up a certain number of Cavalry on the

Sillidaree or contract system. There was, of
course, always the risk of the services of the body
of Horse thus raised being dispensed with by the
state. The value therefore of a Sillidaree assamee
rose or fell according to the belief in the perma-
nency or otherwise of the service. The presence
of British Officers with, and the beneficial arrangements introduced by them into the Nizam's
Horse soon made the service one of much request
amongst natives, and the value of these situations
rose accordingly; but the circumstance which
above all others tended to enhance these appointments in the eyes of native horsemen, and of the
gentry of the country who formed no inconsidera-
ble portion of their Native Officers, was the *faith*
placed in our continuance of the system of permitting these assamees to be held as "property."
No better proof of this can be offered, than the state-
ment of the fact that a certain number of assamees
(according to the means of the family) were and
are constantly assigned over as the ' muhr' or
marriage portion of the daughters of our officers

and men. To introduce any regulation therefore, that would have the effect of shaking this faith, would, I imagine, be extremely unadvisable; for it is evident, that the higher the value set upon his situation by the soldier* the more careful will he be in so conducting himself both in quarters and in the field as not to run the risk of forfeiting it.

I think I have said enough to show, that any interference with the long established rights of Sillidars, " the most important rank in our service" as Col. J. Sutherland truly called them, should if possible be avoided, or at least exercised with extreme caution and delicacy.

But on the other side of the question, there can scarcely be a doubt, that unless some check were put upon the power of the Sillidar to dispose of his horses or assamees, on many occasions, very serious inconvenience to the public service and the efficiency of the horse might arise. To state an extreme, but not impossible case, the whole or a

* Seventeen hundred Rupees is about the average selling price of Sillidaree situations at this time in the Nizam's Service.

large majority of the horses of the various corps
might be purchased by, or bequeathed to a party
or parties ill-disposed to the state, and who might
exercise the influence which a Sillidar possesses,
(and that, in the case of a Sillidar of a large Pagah
is very great) directly in opposition to the Government which pays him. The view which has been
taken of these difficulties by the Officer at present
Commanding the Nizam's Cavalry appears to be
the most judicious. In all cases where the owner of
the Sillidaree assamee *sells* his horses, whether the
sale be in consequence of debts which he is called
upon to pay, or whether it arises from his wish to
leave the service and retire with a certain sum to
his home, it has been ruled that, *for the future*, all
purchasers must be "fighting men" already borne
on our rolls or willing and fit to enter our service.
Nor is this any hardship on the sellers, as there are
numerous parties willing to purchase already in
our ranks, who will pay as high a price as those out
of them. This regulation puts a stop in some
measure to any further increase of that class who

E

own assamees, but do not serve in person. The
right of bequeathment to his widow, son, or other
members of his family has been very wisely and
judiciously left with the Sillidar; and this power,
in those corps where it is not admitted I would
earnestly recommend to be granted. I speak with
the greatest confidence when I assert that, there is
no arrangement which so attaches to the service
and ensures the good conduct of the Native horseman as the above important indulgence.

The Sillidar is the Native 'bhula admee'—his
situation is looked upon as one of the greatest
respectability; and many amongst them,—some of
them cadets of good and noble families—have been
known to serve as privates refusing non-commissioned rank until their standing or their services
entitled them to succeed to the Commissioned
grade. He is the party, who, through the medium
of his superiors, may be said to contract with the
Government, for a certain stipulated sum, to provide an efficient man and horse, a third of this
sum being the almost universal proportion which

is considered the personal pay of the rider. With
the remaining two-thirds he has to feed his horse,
to replace it when cast or dead; and to provide
his own stabling and every single article of horse-
furniture and accoutrements. The only occasion
on which it is customary for the state to assist him
is, when his horse is killed in action, or dies from -
the effects of forced marches on service. In the
Nizam's horse a scale of payment on account of
such casualties is laid down, which is worthy of
attention in all corps of Irregular Cavalry. Suppose a horse entertained when four years of age,
after six years' service, or when he is ten years old,
deduct from his registered value five per cent.

after 7 years' service, or when 11 years old deduct 13 per cent.

„ 8	„	12	„	23	„	
„ 9	„	13	„	35	„	
„ 10	„	14	„	50	„	
„ 11	„	15	„	70	„	

after which he is supposed to have no registered
value. In the corps of Kurnool Horse, in the
Nizam's Cavalry, and, I believe, in the Poonah

Auxiliary Horse, the Sillidar has the right of selecting (except in cases hereafter specified) his Bargheers on the occurrence of any vacancy on his horses, subject of course to the approval of his Commanding Officer. This right of selection is much prized, and naturally; as adding not only to the importance of the Sillidar, but also to his means of providing for the members of his family or his friends. Considering the delicate relation that subsists between the owner of the· horse and its rider, how frequently the latter if not on good terms with the former, can cause him much annoyance and loss, it seems only fair and just that the Sillidar should possess this patronage. The necessity of obtaining the approval of his Officer is a check sufficient to prevent any abuse of this power. If the recruit first brought up is not fit for the service, if in fact, he is not a ready-made horseman and au fait with his weapons, he can be rejected, and the Sillidar desired to bring another. Some limit as to the time requisite to furnish a recruit in, should be fixed, and if within this period he is not brought,

the vacancy can be filled up by the Commanding
Officer.   But it should be a settled point that the
selection rests with the Sillidar, a right which can
only be forfeited by his failing to bring a rider
within a stipulated time.

Vacancies occurring on horses which belong to
the Pagahs of those *not* serving in person should
be· filled up by the European Officer as much as
possible from the relations of Officers and men already in our ranks.

I have before stated that those who object to the
system of Benoka Sillidars, contend also that the
continuance of large Pagahs, the property of one
individual, are injurious to the service.   I admit
generally that large Pagahs are not so well found as
small ones, that a man can better superintend
half-a-dozen horses than half a hundred, and that
it is only natural that he should be more particular
in purchasing a horse for his own riding,· than for
his bargheer: but I consider the advantages of
permitting large and moderate Pagahs far to out-
weigh the objections urged against them.   I
would, in the first instance, look more to the *man*

than to the horse; for I am quite certain, that a
good man on a bad or indifferent horse, will do
much better service than a bad man on a good
nag. I imagine, that by permitting one individual
to possess 10, 20, 50, 100, or more horses, we get
a description of men to enter our ranks who would
never do so if limited to one horse. With the former power, men of noble and of good families will
willingly take service, bringing with them a number of their relations and friends as bargheers; and
I contend that men of this sort are more intelligent,
and are better and more gallant soldiers than the
class of men who would serve as one-horse Sillidars. I say, that it adds to the respectability of
any service which can enumerate in its rolls the
names of many members of good old families and
descendants of warlike chiefs, and also to its popularity. Nay, further I assert, that many and many
a good trooper whose earlier education was probably commenced in the rough school of the " Meer
Khanee"* will take service as Bargheers on the horses

* In the service of the late Nuwab Ameer Khan of Tonk.

of such men, from old feudal, family, or military
feelings who never would otherwise enter our ranks.
But there is, another, a political point of view, in
which the question should be considered. Persons
of the class I mean, members of good and respectable, and, in many instances, of high and noble families have, unfortunately, very few opportunities
of obtaining service under our rule; or rather I
should say there are few situations under our Government which their ancient prejudices and their
pride will suffer them to accept. To the Military
class the Irregular Cavalry is almost the only open-
ing that offers, and it must always be the interest
of Government to provide such means as will
convert dissatisfied and disaffected subjects into
cheerful and well disposed servants;—no measures
tending still more to discourage the entrance of
this class into our service should be entertained,
except on the most clear and unquestionable
grounds. As our rule has extended, this description of men has gradually but steadily receded
before it. Those who had not entered the ranks

of the Irregular Cavalry sought refuge and service in States that still adhered to the old customs they were used to and reverenced. They were to be found thickly interspersed in the forces of Scindiah and the Nizam, many at Nagpore and at Bhopal, at Tonk and some few with the Kurnool Nuwab. Recent changes have made the first and last mentioned powers no longer able to support them as formerly ; and daily as our dominion and interference in the affairs of Native States increases, their chance of obtaining the only sort of service they will accept decreases in like ratio. What is the end naturally to be expected from such causes? One of three results must follow. They must either swallow their prejudice and their pride, and, casting away for ever the recollections of their former state, enter into such service as is free to them —a service which they disgust and loathe as utterly repugnant to their previous habits and feelings; —or they must gradually be *absorbed* by starvation ;—or lastly, as desperate men, reduced to the last extremities, they will join the enemies of our

Government and create or foment disturbances.
The first result all British experience in India
goes to prove highly improbable. Up to this day,
with I suppose scarcely half-a-dozen exceptions,
members of this class have never entered the ranks
of our Regular Army in any branch. The second
is an alternative that the humanity of English
rulers would revolt from :—the third is one which,
it is only natural to suppose, those in authority
would not willingly give occasion for, especially
when feasible means of averting a catastrophe so
much to be deprecated are at hand. If therefore
only as a sort of safety valve, an outlet in the first
instance for turbulent and haughty spirits, who
gradually become better disposed as they find
their interests linked with ours, I would suggest
that in all Native Horse the power of holding considerable Pagahs, as an inducement to men of rank
and respectability to enter our service, should be
continued or introduced where it has not hitherto
been the practice. Taking them all together, in
the Nizam's service, these large Pagahs have not
been worse found than others ; in some instances

F

they are better. In that of Nuwab Murdan Yar
Jung the penurious disposition of the individual
has certainly had this effect,—that his horses and
accoutrements are not generally so good as that of
others: but on the other hand the large body under Ahmed Bukhsh Khan Nagur is superior to
any; and the Pagahs of the late Busalut Jehan, of
Mahomed Shadee Khan, of the son of the late
Bolak Beg Khan, of Mirza Zoolfikar Alee Beg
and his family, of Meer Bundeh Hussun and Meer
Wuzeer Alee Khan Buhadoor may safely be con-
trasted with an equal number of indiscriminately
selected horses belonging to small or one-horse
Sillidars.

One of the chief recommendations of Irregular
Cavalry is, that they are independent of the Commissariat, and are supposed to be able to march at
the shortest notice, without any assistance from
Government, being furnished with carriage and
bazars of their own. In these corps therefore one
Saees and a good and substantial tattoo should be
kept up for every two horses; and it is the duty of
the Sillidar to furnish them,—the maintenance of

both being included in his contract. On the line
of march the pony carries the head and heel-ropes
of the horses, their gram-bags, &c., and the light
bedding and a change or two of raiment for the
two Bargheers. In Cantonment it is employed in
bringing in grass or hay or fire-wood or in any way
the Sillidar may direct. This is a point that
should be well looked to, as the number and good-
ness or otherwise of these tattoos materially affect
the efficiency of a Regiment; but the Sillidar
should not be unnecessarily interfered with in any
arrangements he may make, so long as the duty
required from him is performed. It seldom hap-
pens that any dispute arises between the owner
and the riders of the horses, and when it does, it is
as well to endeavour to let them settle it among
themselves; but as a general rule which may be
enforced on occasions, the weight which each Bargheer may be permitted to carry on the Sillidar's
pony should be limited to 28 lbs. Of Regimental
Bazars, so important to the usefulness of Native
Horse, I shall treat, under that head, hereafter.

CHAPTER IV.

———

Bargheers—the duties of—Recruits, how selected—
the opinion of Col. J. Sutherland—From what
class chosen—Pathans—their feelings of clanship
— Treatment of—Sale of Bargheeree Assamees re-
commended and why.

A TROOPER or officer riding a horse not his own
property is called a 'Bargheer,' and his share of the
Government pay for man and horse is calculated,
almost universally, at one-third of the entire sum.*
From this he should furnish every article of his
uniform, his weapons and his service ammunition.
It should be his duty to see that the horse he rides
is properly fed, shod and groomed, and to repre-
sent any remissness in the first place to his Sillidar,
when, if not attended to, he can carry his complaint to higher authority.

The Bargheer in Irregular Cavalry under British

———

* The officer who may be a Bargheer, of course receives the
whole pay of his rank.

superintendence is much better off than he was when serving Native States. Then it was the usual custom, which could only be departed from with the consent of the Sillidar, to consider his hold on the service to depend upon the life of his horse. Should the horse be killed or sold out of the service, and the owner be unable or unwilling to replace it, the Bargheer's situation was forfeited. This, independent of its injustice, was likely to have a very injurious practical effect. A man knowing his situation dependent on the life of his horse would be chary how he exposed him to risk in action, and an inducement was thus created to hang back in the field. This has been altogether changed, and the Bargheer should be looked upon as entirely a Government servant, whose retention in and dismissal from the service does not rest with the Sillidar. The Bargheer knowing that the continuance of his services does not depend on the life of his horse, and the Sillidar being assured that if the latter is killed in action the Government will reimburse

him its registered value, to go towards providing
another, there can be no considerations of a pecuniary nature to prevent a proper and creditable
performance in the field on the part of either.

It is very difficult to define the best description
of persons to take as recruits into the ranks of
the Irregular Cavalry. The selection must vary
so much under particular circumstances. In corps
that have been long raised, and have become
accustomed to our superintendence, supposing that
the men are what they always should be ' Usharf,' *
it is best to confine your selections as much as
possible to the relations of men already serving
in the corps :—nor does this limit your selection
to any extent, for, in a service so popular as this,
there are numerous candidates for vacancies, who
remain with the Regiment and qualify themselves
for its ranks.† Under other circumstances, such

* Usharf means, in this sense, highly respectable,—above performing menial work, &c. &c.

† Vide report of Captain (now Lt.-Col.) James Blair to Sir
Edward Barnes.

as raising a fresh body of Horse, the object of
the Government in so doing should be borne in
mind; whether it is directed from merely local
considerations, or required only as an increase to
this branch of the army. For instance the motives
for raising Irregular Horse for the late Shah Soojah-
ool-Moolk, and the Corps at Kurnool, were very
different. The former was required for imme-
diate service, the latter was raised chiefly (on
assuming the Government of the Kurnool territo-
ries) to afford means of subsistence to a class of
people which by the deposition of the Newab was
deprived of its livelihood; and also as a political
measure, by which a considerable body of turbulent Patans might be converted from disaffected
idlers with no occupation, into well-disposed servants of the state. It is needless to say more to
prove how different the selection of persons to fill
vacancies would be in such opposite cases.

As a general rule of guidance I cannot do better
than quote the words of Lt.-Col. Sutherland on this
subject, namely, that any man " coming under the

" designation of a Bhula Admee or Ushraf, being a
" horseman and expert in the use of his arms, with
" figure, strength and activity, fit for the duties above
" described, may be admitted at the option of Com-
" mandants." If he answers to the above description, let him be a Mahomedan, a Rajpoot, a Mahratta, or a Seik; although the last race, from what
I have personally experienced of them, are by far
the worst, and do not make good soldiers: I have
ever found them a drunken, boastful, pusillanimous
set. The Mahratta is generally a good horseman,
quick and intelligent, but intriguing and trouble-
some, and not so gallant as the Rajpoot and the
Mahomedan. The military character of the Rajpoot is well known. They are a noble race, but turn
out very few really good horsemen. There are
exceptions of course, and glorious ones; but the
average of good horsemen amongst Rajpoots, I do
not consider to reach more than one in six. This,
however, is not the case if you can procure the
really good specimen of the equestrian genus whose
' habitat' is in Shikawat in Jessulmere, and in parts

of Cutch. Those that I have met with from these
districts come up almost to my 'beau ideal' of a
native Sowar. But the Mahomedans, after all, as
a race, make the best Irregular Cavalry, and of
them again, the Pathan is the first in excellence.
The most superior amongst them are a set of men
now getting almost extinct, who served long in
Native States, and especially with the Nuwab Meer
Khan, and in some of the better " durras" of the
Pindarees. In Upper India, the Pathans of Rampore, Mhow, Shumshabad near Furruckabad, and
Jellalabad near Shajehanpoor, are the best. They
are generally illiterate, haughty and turbulent; but
they are gallant and true, hard-working and zealous, and with even a little kindness and tact in
their management, make such troops as no one
need hesitate to lead where blows are most rife.
I know that many officers dislike both the Mhow
and Rampore men, alleging that they are trouble-
some, and always mixed up in every disturbance,
or Khanu-jungee within reach of them; that they
are overbearing and turbulent, and not much

disposed to be respectful to superiors. My opinion
is that where they run restive, the fault will be
found in the want of tact, or of judgment of the
European Commandant in settling the dispute.
There is amongst the Pathans a strong feeling of
clanship, and they are peculiarly sensitive to the
opinion of their own " Khel or Zye." Send,
therefore, for the offender and the head of his
Khel, the ' boozoorg admee' of his ' buraduree,'
and call them before you.   Point out to the former
firmly, yet calmly, the fault he has been guilty of;
not in " King Cambyses' vein," for there is no
occasion to " do it in passion," but as if " more in
sorrow than in anger."   Let him see what a considerable donkey he is, to risk the loss of his service
which such conduct will infallibly entail.   Then
turning to the " elder," express your regret that he
should have so little influence over his ' bhaee-
bunds' as not to be able to prevent such and such
disgraceful conduct;—that you would be sorry to
publish to the corps at large anything likely to
give a bad name to his party; and therefore, out of

regard for the 'hoormut' of his brethren, you will
give him the opportunity of endeavouring to bring
the offender to his senses, and that so many hours
are permitted with that hope.   Rely upon it, they
will return within the stipulated time; and that a
dispute thus settled, is permanently and well
settled, and will not cause you any annoyance
again.

The Pathan of Shajehanpore is good, and generally better informed and more intelligent than his
brethren from Rampore and Mhow; but he has
somewhat of the Cashmeree in his disposition,
loves intrigue, and has always a hankering after
the "flesh-pots of Egypt," which being interpreted
means to him, Civil situations, Darogaships,
Mohurrurships, Nazirships, &c., in our Revenue
or Judicial departments.

There is a warlike clan of Mussulman, chiefly
Syuds who dwell in Samanah, and about Puttialla,
and around Jheend, &c.   I have known good men
from Mahomedan colonies near Guzerat, and a
large party of Beloochees, now serving in the

Nizam's Cavalry, are not surpassed by any, in all
the qualities which constitute a good trooper.
Hyderabad, Ellichpore, Aurungabad, Kurnool,
Akola, Patoor, Bapim and Mulkapore, are all good
fields for recruiting in the Deccan. But to whatever creed or country irregular horsemen may
belong, it is the *treament* they receive which will
make them either cheerful and zealous soldiers or
useless rabble.   I will again quote the same authority, as one of the highest and best on this point
in India.   " The mode of treatment suited to the
" habits and feelings of the native horseman or Bhu-
" la Admee, is a most important consideration. No
" Soldier in India is more orderly, or more respect-
" ful to his European officers than the Native
" horseman. There is perhaps none whom kindness
" and good treatment will more lead to a gallant
" bearing in presence of an enemy and devotion
" to his officers.   There is none, however, who
" can less bear rudeness or offensive language ;
" and he must never be submitted to either.
" He must feel that he is certain of being well

" received by his officer." * * * * " according
" to his station.   Nothing in treatment or obedi-
" ence should be imposed on, or required of, the
" soldier which may tend to lower him in his
" own estimation, or in that of his fellows in
" or out of the service.   Men who would submit
" to this would not be worth commanding."

An officer who has not had much intimacy with
natives of this description, even with the best
intentions, may unwillingly offend and annoy
them from this very ignorance.   A few general.
directions may, perhaps, be of advantage.   First
After the example of that polished prince who
took off his hat to a street sweeper, because he
would not be outdone by him in politeness, always
return every man's salutation, whatever his rank ;
and on occasions of visits paid to you, request the
visitors to be seated, either on a chair, or on the
ground, according to his standing.   Should the
visitor be a man of high family, or an officer of
high rank, long standing, or distinguished services,
it will not cause you much trouble, and it will

be gratifying to and proper towards him to advance to the door of your house to receive him, and, taking him by the hand, to lead him to a seat and make the usual enquiries after his welfare.

Avoid abuse, which is not only highly insulting to the party at whom it is levelled, but degrading to the utterer, and lowers him beyond belief in the estimation of his men. On occasions when you have to find fault, reflect first, whether the end you wish to obtain may not be better gained by a private (this will, of course, depend on the character of the man and the nature of his offence) than by a public reprimand. On such occasions be very mild but very firm.

The visits of officers of a certain grade (i. e. of native Commandants of Corps and commanders of troops) should be returned on particular occasions, such as the ' Eeds,' or on first arriving at a station after a considerable absence, or when leaving it for some time.

Do not send away from your door a native

gentleman who has taken the trouble of calling on
you, with " Aj foorsut nuheen" or "Sahib aram
kurte :" if you are really so occupied as not to be
able to receive him, have this well explained to
him ; but it is better, if possible, to receive him if
only for a moment, tell him in person why you
have no leisure just then, and appoint some other
time for his visit.

Have nothing to say to their private and domestic affairs if you can avoid it ; you will thus escape
much trouble and considerable ill-well.   There
are occasions when you cannot help listening to,
and granting your interference in such matters ;
but make it a general rule, to which this is to be
only the exception, to induce them to settle their
private affairs amongst themselves.

Do not get into the habit of issuing continued
orders ; when you have to speak, do so to the purpose, and in such a manner as to ensure obedience.
Remember the old story of the boy perpetually
bawling out " Wolf ! wolf !" until no one heeded
him.   " Verbum sap."

Enter as much as possible into the amusements
of your men. Take notice of those who excel as
horsemen, and in the use of their weapons; and
either join in their warlike sports, or at least be a
constant spectator and applauder of them. Encourage them in such pursuits by occasionally giving a
silver "Kurrah" or some other trifle, which the
man who can win may bear off. The article is not
prized for its value, but for the mode in which it
has been obtained.

Be prepared to receive their visits of ceremony,
and the nuzzurs on the various Eeds and festivals;
and be liberal in subscribing your share to the
expense incurred on such occasions. The 'nuzzur'
of a native horseman is, generally, his sword; the
hilt of which is presented to you, which you touch
and embrace the presenter.

Lastly make it a *duty* to know each man by
name; and to keep persons of the same clan or
"kowm," as much as possible together. The system of keeping what are called bhaee-bunds, or
portions of the same sect or clan, as much as possible

in one body, renders the men themselves happier
and benefits the service.   It guards against the
sense (experienced by the *isolated* man) of feeling
alone and deserted if sick or wounded ; and it
promotes good conduct in the field, for the account of misbehaviour, occurring before his brethren and clan, would be conveyed even to the
home of the offender, and render him an object
of scorn in his own village.   I am not one who
believes that the native Soldier, (especially of
the class we recruit from) is dead to shame.   This
arrangement also ensures less trouble in cantonments, for many a slight dispute or trivial quar-
rel which would otherwise run into long enquiries and ' punchayets,' are settled, and better
settled in the ' biraduree' of the clan, in ten
minutes.

It is true, sometimes rivalry between two sects
thus collected into distinct separate bodies might
arise and cause some little trouble ; but a judicious
Commanding Officer would know how to take
advantage of such a feeling, and turn it to the

H

benefit of the service, either in garrison or in the field. A spirit of emulation never yet spoiled a soldier.

Now, all the foregoing directions seem to be very trivial, but it is by such trifles as these, extra of course to your graver duties, that affection is won and regard secured: and the affection and regard of those you command, no one, who has ever experienced the possession or the want of them on the day of strife, will deem a trifle.

There are two regulations in force in the Nizam's Cavalry regarding the Bargheer, the operation of which has been found so beneficial, that permission to introduce them into those bodies of horse where they do not exist, should at once be obtained.

The first is, that "when a Bargheer is killed in action, or shall die after an uninterrupted service of ten years, it shall be incumbent on the Sillidar to fill up the vacancy by a duly qualified member of the Bargheer's family."

The second is " After fifteen years' service, old

men shall have the privilege of retiring from the
service, and giving a son or near relation (duly
qualified) in their stead."

.The corps of Irregular Cavalry on the Bengal
establishment are admitted to the benefit of the
pension establishment. The corps of Horse at
Kurnool, and the Nizam's Cavalry have no retiring
pension ;—the introduction of the following 'suggestion is, therefore, more desirable in the two
latter than in the former services; although its
universal adoption in all corps of Irregular Cavalry
would, I think, be highly beneficial. I advance
this suggestion of mine, however, with hesitation,
as I know that some, and one officer in particular,
of high standing and great experience with native
Horse, for whose opinion I have much respect,
differ from me in the view I have taken on this
subject. My proposal is, that the situations of
Bargheers, the ' Bargheeree assamees,' as they are
called, should be permitted, with certain restric-
tions, to be bought and sold, as Sillidars in the
Nizam's service are allowed to do with their

Assamees, and as Officers in Her Majesty's service are authorized to sell their commissions.

In two Regiments belonging to the Nizam's Cavalry Brigade this system of permitting Bargheers to sell their situations on retiring from the service, was tolerated, although never expressly sanctioned by Government. The system now recommended has certainly many advantages ; and the only plausible argument I have heard against it is, that it involves the recruit who purchases into the service in debt, at first starting. But from what I have learnt of the practical operation of this indulgence in the two regiments where the system prevailed for a considerable period, I consider the objection altogether groundless. In a large majority of instances the owner of the horse on which the vacancy occurred, or his family, advanced the money to the Bargheer who retired, to secure the situation for some relative of their own. It is worth the Sillidar's while to give a better price than any other party, as he secures his own relative on his own horse, a great object with him. Where this was not the case, the friends and relations of the party wishing to purchase in, clubbed the necessary sum. It is their interest also to do so, for the candidate was, most probably, a drain upon their resources; and by paying down a certain sum, and once starting him in life, they considered he had no further claim upon them. Under no circumstances was the sum required borrowed, for the price that these situations generally realized was about four hundred rupees; and what Sahookar would advance that sum which was to bear interest at 12 per cent per annum, upon promise of repayment at the rate of $7\frac{1}{2}$ rupees per mensem? the maximum amount of instalment that a Sowar is permitted to assign. Past experience and all probability go to prove then, that the candidate could not and did not involve himself by purchasing his situation. Let us look at the other side of the question. The advantages to the old soldier who wishes to retire are clear and undeniable. The sale of his situation gives him a small sum of money to take to his home, which, if properly laid

out, may render the few remaining years of his
life comfortable and respectable. This would be
desirable even where pensions are granted ; but it is
still more so in a service having no such advantage.
The benefit to the State is also, I think, equally
manifest. The man who stakes four hundred rupees
for his situation, will naturally reflect more before
he commits himself by misconduct entailing the loss
of that situation, than one who obtained his place
for nothing. The latter loses his service alone,
which he may obtain again elsewhere; the former
not only his berth but his coin also, and natives
are certainly *as much* influenced by pecuniary considerations as we are. In any view of the case
it is a security given, to the extent of four hundred
rupees, for the good conduct of the private soldier,
which we have not now. There can be no harm
in obtaining this security, especially when gained
without expense to the state, and at the same time
providing a retiring ' bonus' to the old and wornout soldier.

No man of course should be permitted to sell

except after a certain number of years' service, or
from being unfit ; in short without the sanction of
his commandant; which would be a sufficient check
to any possible abuse of the indulgence.   If the objection to the plan that I have above stated is valid,
is it not probable that it would have been urged
against the purchase of commissions in the Royal
service ; the principle of each being nearly similar?

In 1841 when I was placed at the disposal of
the Government of Fort St. George, and raised
the corps which now is known by the name of the
Kurnool Horse, there were at the time certain
objections of a local nature to the introduction of
this regulation, and accordingly I did not then
propose its adoption.   From what I have learnt
since, these do not now exist, and as that corps,
as well as the Cavalry of H. H. the Nizam has
no pension establishment, the arrangement now
recommended would be especially desirable there,
although as before stated, I am of opinion that its
general adoption would be found to be beneficial
in all corps of Irregular Cavalry.

CHAPTER V.

Pay, Rates of, in Nizam's Cavalry, Kurnool Horse and Hindostan Irregular Cavalry. The Sherra of 20 rupees insufficient—Case in point. Scheme for raising the " Sherra" in the Hindostan Corps. Table of average weight carried.

———

. IT is difficult exactly to determine what is sufficient pay to support troops in a condition to be at all times fit for service, to march at the shortest notice, complete in horses, arms, appointments and bazars, without requiring any aid from the Government, or any further assistance from the country through which they pass, than their own bazars and purses can command. This is the essential point in a corps of Irregular Cavalry, and in this consist their efficiency and advantage over other troops, that they are entirely independent of the commissariat.

To obtain this desirable object, their pay must

be handsome.   The two following tables shew the
rate of pay of each rank in the Nizam's Cavalry,
and in the Irregular Cavalry of Hindostan.

No. I.*—Nizam's Cavalry.

1 Riseldar†	500	1 Trumpeter	40
1 Jemadar	200	1 Kettle Drummer	40
1 Duffadar	60	1 Camel Gunner	30
1 Naib, ditto	50	1 Regimental Mootsud- dee	50
1 Trooper { Bargheer 15 Sillidar 25 }	40	1 Troop ditto	20
1 Trumpeter Major	50		

No. II.—Irregular Cavalry of Hindoostan.

	Pay of each rank.	Total of each rank.
1 Woordie Major	105	
1 Nukeeb	20	
1 Ressaldar	150	
1 Ressaidar	80	
1 Naib Ressaldar.	50	
1 Jemadar	45	
1 Kote Duffadar	35	
1 Duffadar	28	
1 Nishanburdar	28	
1 Trumpeter	25	
1 Kettle Drummer	25	
1 Trooper { Bargheer 6 10 0 Sillidar 13 6 0 }	20	

* The above Table is for Hyderabad Rupees, which, at the Govt.
rate, is 21 per cent. less than the Company's Rupees.

† In the Nizam's Cavalry there is but one Rissaldar to each
regiment, in the Hindostan T. C. there are four. The Nizam's
troops are also four, or four and a half months in arrears of pay.

I

These Tables shew the highest and the lowest
scale of pay. The Poonah Horse are not all paid
alike, the "Sherra" or rate of pay for one trooper
and his horse varying from 20 up to, I believe, 30
Co.'s Rs., those drawing the higher rate having
either been transferred from Skinner's Horse, or
raised at an earlier date than the rest of the Regiment.

In the Kurnool Horse the sherra is 25 Co.'s
Rupees and the pay of the various ranks as follows:

No. III.—Kurnool Horse.

	Pay of each rank.
1 Rissaldar	300
1 Jemadar	150
1 Naib ditto	100
1 Duffadar	50
1 Naib ditto	35
1 Trooper .... { Bagheer .. 8 5 4 { Sillidar .. 16 7 8	25
1 Trumpeter	25
1 Kettle Drummer	25
1 Sudder Moonshee	30
1 Troop Mutsuddee	12-8

The pay of the Nizam's trooper is handsome,*

* Equal to Co.'s Rs. 33-0-11.

enables him to keep up good appointments, and a very superior horse, and gives him on an average a yearly profit of sixty rupees.* That of the Kurnool trooper would barely remunerate him, (considering the *expensive* country he lives in) were it not that he is stationary and escapes all the various losses which constant moving entails. The pay of the Hindostan trooper is not enough, and he cannot mount himself as he ought to be mounted, nor live as he should live. I consider Company's rupees 30 per mensem, a fair pay for each man and horse, of which the Sillidar should receive 20, and the Bargheer 10 rupees. That this is not too high a rate, I think the subjoined table will prove, premising, that I take the average cost of each horse to be 200 Rupees,† an average rather under than above a fair one.

---

* 60 Hyderabad Rs.— 49-9-5 Company's.

† The average cost of Remounts in the Nizam's Cavalry is 383-5-8 Hyderabad Rupees.

No. IV.

	Per Annum.		
Original cost of horse			200
12 per Cent. on his Capital	24	0	0
Wear and tear of the Horses* calcu-) lated to last 10 years ....)	20	0	0
Gram 4 0 0			
Forage 3 0 0			
Saees (proportion) 2 8 0			
Shoeing 1 0 0			
Stabling, Clothing, Head) and heel ropes, &c. ..) 1 0 0			
11 8 0by12=	138	0	0
Saddle and Horse appointments........	12	0	0
Wear and tear of a tattoo and propor-) tion of grain and forage for it, &c. ..)	24	0	0
Total	218	0	0
12 Months' pay at 20 per mensem	240	0	0
Sillidar's yearly profit	22	0	0

I believe there is little doubt, and the fact will be admitted by officers of the Irregular Cavalry of Hindoostan, that the sherra of 20 rupees is perfectly inadequate for the support of an efficient horse and man. As a body the Hindoostan corps are very poorly mounted, and were it not that service for the class of men composing Irregular Cavalry is so exceedingly scarce, few would be

---

* The average length of service is under nine years.

found to agree to a contract on such terms. It is, as I have before observed, a popular service, but its popularity arises not from its pecuniary advantages, but, because it is the only service under our rule which squares with the tastes and prejudices of the " Ushraff," and which they do not think it derogatory to their respectability—their *izzut* to enter.

I remember in 1839 when the Government of Bombay wished to increase the Poona Horse by an auxiliary levy, upon a reduced sherra similar to that of the Hindoostan Irregular Corps (viz. 20 rupees), I was requested to assist the officer then in charge of the Poona Horse at Seroor by raising a troop at Mominabad—I did so. The whole party was composed of highly respectable men, relations chiefly of troopers, &c., in the Nizam's Horse, who, finding they could not get an entrance there, from there being no vacancies, and feeling that they were a burden upon the slender resources of their relatives, accepted service upon the reduced pay. On their arrival at Seroor many of them were promoted, yet, notwithstanding, several returned to me after six or eight months' absence, having disposed of their assamees, including the horse, at a less price than the original cost of the animal itself, because they discovered, that by contracting to keep up an effective horse, and to clothe, arm, and equip themselves they were considerable losers.

The difference of a few rupees in the pay for each man and horse will just make the difference between obtaining the services of *Cavalry* efficient in every sense, and of a mounted rabble, barely fit for even Police duties, who as they lack the means of keeping up externally a respectable appearance, so do they lose their self-respect, and become dispirited, crippled, and useless.

The Tables Nos. I. and II. shew that there is a great difference in the various grades commissioned and non-commissioned of the Hindoostan and Nizam's Cavalry. It appears to me that the distinctions of rank in No. I. are more simple and therefore preferable to those of No. II. No. III.

has the advantage of the intermediate step between Jemadar and Duffadar, between an increase
of pay from 60 to 200 rupees; which, as I
deemed it advisable, I introduced into the Kurnool Horse.

The more simple the composition of Irregular
Cavalry the better; and, as I hereafter shall attempt to shew, the various ranks enumerated in
No. L seem to provide for all the necessary duties.
I introduce the subject here to point out that by
abolishing a number of useless grades and increas-
ing the sherra of the private, a much greater degree
of efficiency might be obtained in the Irregular
Corps of Hindoostan without any considerable increase of expense.

Exclusive of pay for European Officers in both
instances, the total cost of a Corps of Nizam's
Cavalry numbering 550 fighting men, including
the expense of establishment and four Camel-
guns attached to each Corps is 25,248 Hyderabad rupees, equal to Co.'s Rs. 20,866-1-9¼.
The amount of the abstract of an Irregular

Corps in Hindoostan consisting of 645 fighting
men (including establishment) is Rs. 15,219-0-0
per mensem.

Difference in Co.'s Rs. 5,647-1-9½.

But this difference does not include the expense
to the Company's Government for pensions to
the Hindoostan Irregular Horse, an item which,
I imagine, will be found nearly to equalize the
cost of both corps ; in which case, that Government pays the same price for a very inferior description of force, although numerically stronger by
80 troopers per Regiment.

Those who have seen Regiments of both services
of the Nizam's Cavalry and of the Irregular Horse
of Hindoostan—cannot hesitate in admitting the
infinite superiority of the former. The average
price of remounts, in the latter is, as far as I have
been able to learn, about 160 Co.'s Rupees : that
of the Nizam's Cavalry is Hyderabad Rs. 383-5-8
equal to Co.'s 316-13-2. In the essential point
of horses, therefore, there is nearly a difference of
2 tt 1, and unless it is proved that an equally good

horse can be procured in Upper India at half the
price, it must be admitted that the Nizam's Horse
are better mounted; for a·higher price will naturally procure a better article. My experience leads
me to believe that there is no difference in the
price of horses in the Deccan and Upper India;
that a horse costing 400 rupees here, would
fetch the same price there; and *vice versâ*. If
this conclusion is correct, the Nizam's Horse
should be, as I believe it is, nearly twice as well
horsed as the Irregular Cavalry of Hindostan. In
the same proportion the pay being handsomer,
superior accoutrements and furniture are insisted
on, and the whole service is better and more efficient in every respect. This higher degree of
efficiency in horses and accoutrements, and advantage to the officers and men, might be obtained by
Government for the Hindostan Irregular Cavalry,
at an increase of 5,761 rupees per mensem; the
numerical superiority of 80 troopers being still
preserved; or if the strength of the regiments
should be equalized with those of the Nizam's

K

Cavalry, at an increase of 3,361 rupees per mensem, as follows:

No. V.

	Pay of each rank.	Total of each rank.
1 Rissaldar at	300	300
8 Jemadars at	150	1,200
16 Duffadars at	50	800
64 Naib ditto at..................	40	2,560
1 Trumpeter Major at............	40	40
6 Trumpeters	30	180
2 Kettle Drummers at	30	60
528 Troopers at	30	15,840
Total cost of proposed arrangement		20,980
Ditto ditto of present ditto		5,219
Difference		5,761
If the number be reduced to the strength of the Nizam's Cavalry, viz. 448 Troopers, deduct 80 Troopers at 30=	2,400	2,400
And the monthly difference will be ..		3,361

This monthly difference of 3,361 Rupees will surely be considered small if put in the scale against the immense advantage which the state will derive from the very superior description of Cavalry, which a sherra of 30 rupees would create.

From the reduced pay of 20 rupees per month,

13-6, of which only the Sillidar receives, he furnishes as good a horse as can be expected from him. We have seen that the average price paid by the Hindostan Khooduspah is considerably under 200 rupees. I subjoin a table shewing the average weight the horses have to carry, and I think it would be difficult indeed in any part of India to purchase horses up to 13½ stone for the sum that they can afford to give.

No. VI.

	St.	lbs	oz.	St.	lbs	oz.
Average weight of men*	8	13	8			
ARTICLES.						
Blanket	0	5	0			
Boots and Spurs	0	2	4			
Cap	0	1	8¼			
Coat	0	2	12¾			
Kummerbund	0	1	0			
Matchlock	0	7	11½			
Pouch, Belt and 10 rounds (Pistol)	0	1	8½			
Ditto, ditto and 60 do. (Matchlock)	0	2	10¼			
Powder Horn and 1¼ lbs. of powder	0	2	8			
Pantaloons	0	1	14			
Lance and Pistol	0	6	0			
Sabre and Belt	0	3	3			
Saddle, Bridle, &c.	2	3	4			
Total of Matchlock-men ..	..	..	..	4	5	11
Ditto of Lancers	..	..	..	4	0	6½

* The average weight carried by horses in the Nizam's Cavalry is 13½ stone. The above is the average of the 3d Irregular Cavalry.

The feats that have been performed by Native Horse when we consider the pay they receive and the manner in which they are mounted are perfectly wonderful : but such officers as have served with them alone know how cruelly a campaign impairs the efficiency of their Regiments, how severe are the individual losses suffered by the Khooduspas, and what a long period of quiet, and in a cheap country, it requires to enable them to recover. Those who saw the 3rd and 4th Regiments of Irregular Cavalry after the campaign in Afghanistan* witnessed how these corps were disabled, although they received, whilst beyond the Indus, an increase to their pay of nearly one-third. Were the alteration in the formation and the increase of their pay, which I have suggested, introduced, the corps of Irregular Horse would be found perfectly equal to any description of duty which could possibly be

* The Irregular Cavalry was most unfairly worked on detachment duties, treasure parties, &c. ; especially that excellent corps the 4th Irregular Cavalry, which notwithstanding it had gone through the first campaign, had, from being quartered at Ferozepore, as many I suppose, as 300 men absent in Afghanistan and traversing the Punjab, &c.

required from really good cavalry ; a fact that
has been proved by the services of the Nizam's
Horse, composed in a great measure of the same
class of men, and owing their superiority only to a
scale of pay which, being handsome without being
exorbitant, enables the British Commandant,
without any cumpunctions of conscience, to insist
upon a liberal fulfilment of the contract, on the
part of the Sillidar, towards the Government
which pays him liberally.

CHAPTER VI.

Duties of Rissaldar—Jemedar—Duffadar, Naib Duffadar, and Private—Arms, Ammunition, Bazaars, Clothing, Discipline, Discharge, Horses, Orderlies, Orders, Punchayuts, Punishments, Promotions, Relief.

I HAVE before stated, that the more simple the formation of a Regiment of Native Horse the better ; that laid down in Table No. I. is one well suited to such a service. I am myself of opinion that the intermediate rank between Duffadar and Jemadar, namely, that of Naib-Jemadar, as stated in Table No. III. is very advantageous ; not only as holding out an extra well-paid situation as a *prize* in the service, but also because the Troop leader or Jemadar should have some Naib or Assistant in every way capable of performing his duties when he himself might be absent, from sickness, on duty, or on furlough.

The various duties of each grade may be thus briefly described.

The Rissaldar is the Native Commandant of the Corps. He has the general superintendence of the internal management of his Regiment. It is to him that the pay of the entire corps is issued. He is the usual channel of communication with the European Commandant, and the keeper of all the Native records, for which he is responsible. He should be a man of considerable influence, of good family, education, and conduct ; in short, a person to be looked up to, respected, and promptly obeyed by all his Native Officers and men.

It should be the object of the European Officer Commanding to make him of some consideration in the eyes of his men : for which purpose a guard should be allowed him at his quarters ; and when proceeding on leave or on duty. Some degree of authority for reward and punishment, should be vested in him ; and his recommendations, if not grossly biassed, should be attended to, or, at all events, received with courtesy.

The Jemadar or Troop leader is the " Captain"
of his troop, and is responsible for its internal
economy, the condition of the horses, arms and
appointments. The less he is interfered with in
the management of his Troop the better, and the
greater pride he will take in its efficiency and
good order. He is responsible for the pay of all
in his Troop, and it is in his presence that the
Troop Mootsuddee disburses it, taking the receipt
of each man separately in the Troop acquittance
roll book kept for that purpose. He should have
authority also to punish slight Military offences
and to grant certain indulgences of leave or ex-
emption from duty in his troop. He should be
a man of great respectability and general intelli-
gence, for much depends on the character of men
in this important grade.

Each Troop should be divided into four Duffas
or divisions, and a Duffadar should be posted to
every two Duffas, for the condition and discipline
of which they should be answerable to the Troop
Commanders. They should report any irregu-
larity or deficiency ; and the junior Duffadar of

the squadron should be selected to carry the standard.

The above should be Commissioned Officers, Naib Duffadars are non-commissioned, and should be considered as aids to the Duffadars—two being attached to each duffa or division. It should also be their especial duty to warn the men for duty, and to enforce their attendance. Sixty-four Naib Duffadars seem a large number for one regiment of Irregular Horse, but when it is remembered how much these Regiments are liable to detachment duties, it will not be found to be more than is absolutely requisite.

Privates may be divided into two classes, Sillidars and Bargheers, but both perform every duty of a Trooper, except in cases where the Sillidar is the owner of six horses, when he should be excused all *dismounted* sentry duties. In promotion, when claims are nearly equal, the preferrence should be given to the Sillidar, not only as being generally the more respectable man, but as having the greater *stake* in the service.

L

Their interest is the best guarantee for their
good conduct, and dismissal in their case,
especially if followed by the dismissal of their
horses also, is so serious a loss that such
punishment will not be lightly risked. In
stating that both Sillidars and Bargheers
should perform every duty expected from
Troopers, one exception should be made. They
should neither ever be required to clean or rub
down their horses, but on most emergent cases on
service when the saees entertained for this pupose
cannot keep up with the troops. The native
horseman has a great objection to this, (in his opinion,) menial labour which he considers unsuited
to his character of " Bhula Admee." As a groom*
should be kept up for every two horses to perform
this work and procure forage, as is the case in the
Nizam's Horse, a system so offensive to their prejudices might with advantage be discontinued.

* A Sillidar of only one horse has to keep up a saees and tattoo
for it separately ; and one saees and one tattoo are attached to
the horse ridden by any officer commissioned or non-commissioned.

No good horseman, whatever his rank, will ever
object to perform this labour which he knows to be
so essential to the comfort and well being of his
horse on occasions of emergency, and on service.
No man who has ever been employed in any menial capacity, or as a private servant should ever
be entertained in the ranks of Irregular Cavalry.

ARMS.—All arms are provided by the soldier
himself, and in the purchase of them he should be
allowed free option.   Every officer, commissioned
or non-commissioned, should have a good sabre
and a pair of pistols—every private a sabre, and
either a matchlock, carbine or lance, as the one or
the other is the most effective weapon in his hand.
Those who carry lances should have one pistol also.
Each man should have either in his spare holster
or attached to his saddle an iron picqueting peg,
and a spare horse shoe.   Twenty-four rounds of
ball cartridge for each carbine or matchlock, and
twelve rounds for each pistol, should always be in
the pouch.   In many regiments of Irregular Horse
the proportion of fire-arms is extravagant.   All

fire arms (except the pistol) are nearly useless to the
trooper when mounted, and those who have seen
much of their mounted practise will bear me out
in this opinion. Ten Carbineers or Matchlockmen
to be disposed at each flank of every squadron is
amply sufficient for all practical purposes. These
men should be prepared to act as skirmishers, and
on an occasion of hill warfare, in jungle, or in the
attack of walled villages or small fortresses, to
dismount and lodge themselves in such places
as will enable them to keep down the fire of the
enemy from walls or elsewhere, (they, themselves
being as much as possible under cover) until
the preliminaries for an assault by the rest of the
corps are arranged. The pistol, as is well known,
is only useful at very close quarters or in extremi-
ty; and a sling for it should be attached to each
Trooper's sword belt on which it should be secured
before going into action. If kept in the holster
pipe, and the Trooper is separated from his horse,
the use of his weapon is lost.

Of all weapons in the hands of a good native

horseman, even superior to the sabre, the native lance, of light but tough bamboo, about nine feet long, is the best. It is more especially useful in difficult country or in brushwood.

There should in every Regiment of Irregular Cavalry be fifty lancers to every ten carbineers.

AMMUNITION.—All *service* ammunition (purchased from Government) should be furnished by the men themselves. Practice ammunition and blank cartridge for breaking in Remounts should be indented for and defrayed by Government.

BAZARS.—It should be the peculiar pride, as it is one of the principal advantages of every Regiment of Irregular Cavalry, to be able to move at the shortest notice, provided with all necessaries, and without any assistance from the Commissariat. To enable each corps separately to do this, there should, besides the arrangement before mentioned, be a distinct Bazar attached to every Regiment over which the Commandant should possess exclusive control, and in the management of which no

Station police master, or Sudder bazar master should be allowed to interfere.

These bazars, if properly managed, not only pay their own expenses, but from the surplus revenue, afford the means of granting donations to wornout men, laid down in page 84, as well as of meeting all the ordinary contingent expenses of the Regiment to which they are attached.

The establishment of these bazars should not cost more than 79 rupees, viz.

		Per Mensem.
1	Cutwal	30
1	Mootsuddee	14
2	Dundiahs	16
1	Hurkarah	6
3	Dhaliahs	12
	Stationery	1
		79

The ordinary management of a regimental bazar is too well known to render it necessary for

me to enter into detail here. The principal points
to be insisted on are, that each bunneeah, &c.,
should be desired to give a written agreement to
keep up a certain number of tatoos and bullocks,
prepared for marching, according to the extent of
his business; and that no nerrick should be forced
but suffered to find its own level which will gene-
.rally be a fair one, if due regard is paid to the
quantity of grain on hand; of which, never less
than fifteen days' consumption should always be
in the bazar.

The contract for the revenues of this regimental bazar, divided under four heads which include
every description of tax, should each be separately
sold to the highest bidder;* from whom a security
to the extent of one-fourth should be taken.

At the end of each month he should pay the
amount of his contract for that month to the
Cutwal.

* The average sum realized by the sale of the contract for the
Regiment of Nizam's Cavalry at Head Quarters, is above 4000
Rupees per annum.

These heads are differently termed in various parts of India. In the Deccan they are called first, Keranee, second, Kullallee, third, Sendhee, fourth, Dundiah.

The first includes the shop tax, every description of European articles, spices, clothes, &c.

The second is the Abkaree for arrack, spirits, &c., and includes courtezans, musicians, &c.

The third is chiefly peculiar to the Deccan, the Sendhee being an intoxicating drink like the toddy in Bengal.

The fourth is in lieu of the usual fees of the Chowdree and bazar servants, amounting to a quarter of a seer for each ; viz., one quarter for the Chowdree, and one for the servants upon every load of grain brought into the bazar. As the bazar servants are proposed to be paid at a fixed rate by Government, the right of collecting these fees should be sold to the contractor, and becomes a source of revenue.

Lastly, the Commanding Officer should endeavour to establish a market day once a week, to which the surrounding villagers should be induced to come to sell their produce.

Upon the existence of a good and well-managed bazar, properly provided with carriage cattle, sufficient for the wants of the Regiment, depends most materially the efficiency of a corps of Irregular Horse.

CLOTHING.—There are a number of most absurd and ill-suited uniforms in vogue for the different regiments of Irregular Cavalry, and great improvement in this respect might be made. The principal points to be borne in mind are, first, cheapness, for the means of the soldier who provides his own dress are small:—secondly, durability;—and thirdly, an absence of all tawdriness and useless glitter. The chief duties the Irregular horseman is likely to be employed on, are, escorts, out-posts, flanking parties, long marches, with the view of taking the enemy by surprize, sudden attacks, &c. The plainer his dress is rendered the easier all this will be effected. The dress of Irregular Cavalry should be entirely *native*, and suited to their own tastes

M

and habits. An Ulkhaluk of any dark coloured cloth, a native turban, black belt, and long boots is the best costume. Fancy dresses should be eschewed. The men should always be permitted to buy their own clothing wherever they please. The Commanding Officer who in his zeal for the good appearance of his regiment assists his men by procuring cloth, &c. from Europe or the presidency, generally performs a thankless part. Even when the most clear accounts are produced before them, natives will think you have had some interest in the commission; that your uncle, perhaps, is a cloth merchant, or your grandmother a dealer in patent leather.

DISCIPLINE.—As I have before observed, a considerable degree of authority should be vested in the native commandant and Troop-leader. They should be taught to consider themselves responsible for their respective charges, and encouraged to take a pride in their commands.

The European commandant, although interfering as seldom as possible, should still narrowly watch their conduct, and his doors should always be open to receive those who may come to consult with or to complain to him. He himself should be so supported always, as to be able to carry all measures with a high hand.

The duties of a corps of this kind are simple, and no great degree of exactness in manœuvre is expected. They should be made efficient as advance or rear guards, or flankers, cutting off supplies, posts and detachments, and as skirmishers, to advance and charge in line, and to change position in column or echellon with rapidity and exactness. They should be fit to take their place in line with Regular Regiments when required. From the complete command which each trooper has over his horse, and from having generally such very intelligent and well educated men as native officers, it is surprizing how soon this degree of efficiency is acquired. Horse exercise for purposes of manœuvre should not be ordered more than five or six times a month; but every possible inducement should be held out to encourage the men to ride their horses frequently, and to practise all the usual native feats of arms and horsemanship.

There should be no foot parade except for occasional inspection of arms, accoutrement, and horse appointments, and no "school" or drill; for, no trooper should be entertained who is not fit to proceed on duty the moment after.

DISCHARGE.—Any man requiring his discharge, should receive it at once, unless under peculiar exigencies. In corps having no pension establishment, old and worn out men, when discharged, should receive donations from the regimental bazar fund, or other source, as follows, agreeably to the rule which obtains in the Nizam's Cavalry.

To men who have served 20 years and upwards 90 Rs.

„	15	„	70 „
„	10	„	50; „
„	7	„	40 „

Where the soldier is disabled by wounds

received on service, it is the *duty* of every Government to pension him.

HORSES.—No horse should be discharged until the owner has had three months' warning. If at the expiration of that time, the place has not been filled up, the 'Assamee' should be given to another.

On the death or sudden disqualification of a horse, two months should be allowed to the Sillidar to provide another, the owner drawing full pay for one month. No horse should be discharged, unless entirely unfit for the service.

No horse should be entertained under 14 hands or under 3½ years of age: nor should any mares be admitted into a regiment.

The Sillidar should procure or purchase his horse wherever he pleases; and if approved of by the commandant, it should be immediately registered,—certifying age, height, colour, marks, caste, price, and date of entertainment.

It is difficult to decide what is the best description of horse for irregular troops. The

genuine Kattywar breed is now seldom seen,
and the real " Deccanee," since the breaking up
of the Mahrattas, has become scarce. Perhaps this
latter is the best description of remount : he is
generally small, about 14-1, but stout and com-
pactly made, particularly well limbed, has high
courage and great powers of endurance. They are
bred chiefly on the banks of the Bheema, and in
the Man-jungles. In the Nizam's service, (from
the neighbourhood of most of the stations to
Bombay,) a number of Arabs have been introduced. The following return shews the proportion
of different castes in the five Regiments of the
Nizam's Horse :

Total Strength 2735.

Arabs	358	Herat	1
Deccanee	1554	Kattywar	4
Hindostan	298	Khelat	1
Wullayutee	79	Not known	375
Persian	58	Wanting to complete	7

Should a horse be killed or incurably injured in
action, or die, or be incurably injured on a forced

march, the owner should receive his registered
. price from the Government, subject to the reduc-
tions mentioned in page 27.

A " Chundah" or Horse Fund to assist Sillidars
in providing remounts, is an admirable arrangement in corps of Irregular Cavalry, if it is established with the entire concurrence of the men.
To effect this, the Sillidars must agree to pay a
certain monthly subscription for each horse ; from
which general fund a settled sum is to be given to
the owner of every horse that *dies*.   If the benefit
is to be extended to the owners of horses that are
cast, calculations must be made accordingly, and
the amount of subscription for each horse must be
considerably increased.   The sum to be given from
this fund to each Sillidar, whose horse has died or
been cast, to assist him in purchasing another,
will, of course, depend upon several contingencies
as, the rate of pay, the amount of subscription to
the Fund, the average price of horses entertained,
the strength of the regiment, &c. &c.

In a regiment consisting of five hundred and

forty-six horses, it appears from calculations which have been made, reaching over a number of years, that the average of remounts admitted annually to replace horses that have died or been cast, is fifty-two,* or a fraction more than four and quarter horses per mensem. To allow for the extra casualties, which active service, or sickly seasons may cause, calculations should be framed for four and half per mensem, or fifty-four horses annually. The sum of 250 rupees from the Fund to assist the Sillidars in purchasing a remount is sufficient. Rupees 200 per horse, for fifty-four horses, 13,500 rupees per annum, to obtain which sum, a monthly subscription of Rs. 2-0-11—60½ per horse must be collected.

Per mensem.   *Per annum.*

For each horse Rs. 2-0-11. 60½ $\times$ 12 = 2-4-11-7 25 $\times$ 546 = Rs. 13,500 with a fraction over.

This draft of a Fund is however calculated for corps when the sherra is 40 rupees per mensem,

---

* Vide note, page 60, giving the average services of horses as under 9 years.

and the average price of remounts 435 rupees.
When the pay is smaller, and the average price of
remounts lower, the scale of subscription, as well
as the sum given from the Fund, must, of course,
be greatly reduced, for if this latter is not considerably *below* the usual price of the remount,
the Sillidar may become careless of his horse, feeling that in the event of a casualty happening, the
amount to be received from the " Chunda" will
reimburse his loss, or nearly so.*

ORDERLIES.—Dismounted Orderlies should never be employed in Irregular Cavalry, the
duties of which should be performed by regimental hurkarahs, and mounted orderlies should
be sparingly used, as the sum given to the Sillidar
for keeping a horse is not sufficient to enable
him to provide horses for the severe duties on
which mounted orderlies are sometimes employed
in the Regular Cavalry.

ORDERS.—All orders should be issued in the

* The accounts of this Fund should be kept by a committee
of native officers.

N

native language. The regimental order being forwarded to the Rissaldar, Jemadars or troop officers send their respective troop mootsuddies or writers with the troop order book into each of which copies are made, and explained by the troop officers to their men.

PUNCHAYUTS.—Regiments of Irregular Cavalry should not be subject to the "Articles of War"; but all offenders should be tried by punchayuts, a system which answers equally well, and is more consonant to their habits. If an offender belonging to an Irregular Regiment is brought to trial before a Detachment or General Court Martial composed, we may suppose, chiefly of officers of the line, who are ignorant of the usages of his corps, he, not unnaturally, conceives that he has not obtained impartial justice.

The following rules, chiefly in accordance with those laid down for the guidance of the Nizam's Cavalry, will be found advantageous :—

The punchayut may consist of 5, 7, or more, or any uneven number including the President.

The authority convening the punchayut should furnish written instructions to the president or " Surpunj," giving in the name or names of the person or parties to be tried, stating the offence or subject of enquiry, and also whether sentence is to be pressed or not.

The prisoner may object to any member or members and to the nature of the proceedings :—effect must be given to the objection at the time, or it must be recorded, with the reasons for over-ruling it.

The proceedings should be conducted as much as possible in conformity with the native rules of evidence and the religion and laws of the *defendant;* and they should be recorded in the native language.

The president, members and witnesses should be put an oath on matters of importance, or when such is the desire of the person whose character or property may be involved in the sentence.

All camp followers should be subject to the same tribunal.

The most serious, indeed almost the only punishment should be dischargè from the service. In cases where a Sillidar is the offending party, he may, according to the nature of the fault, be dimissed, together with his horses—or he may be allowed to dispose of, or to retain them.

The system of stoppages from pay, is, in my opinion, injudicious, although it has been introduced in many' intances. The objection is, that whenever made, the European Officer, amongst the ignorant (who always form the great majority,) has the credit of appropriating the difference to himself; and, in a service where so much depends on individual character, and the respect borne towards superiors, I would leave no door open for suspicion, however unjust or absurd.

The other punishments may be deprivation of leave of absence, stoppage of promotion, reduction to the ranks, or reprimand in front of his troop or regiment; where, in extreme cases, when it may be considered necessary to dismiss the horseman with disgrace, his sword should be broken over his head, and his ulkhaluk torn from his back.

PROMOTION.—Should go by merit; when that is equal, the senior, of course, should be preferred. Where both claims and length of service are nearly balanced, the Sillidar should be chosen before the Bargheer as having a greater stake in the service.

Selection for the commissioned grades should be made from the whole regiment, but the non-commissioned promotions should be confined to the troop as much as possible.

The sons and relations of old and distinguished officers and soldiers of high family should be excused all dismounted sentry duties, and as soon as they prove themselves worthy of it, should be rapidly advanced in the service. This is especially desirable when the young lad may be the head of a clan or party, the older members of which would rather see him established in the rank which his father may have held, than obtain any advantages for themselves.

RELIEFS.—Reliefs should not take place, unless there is an absolute necessity, more than once in four years. It is these constant changes that involve the native officers and men so greatly in debt.

The preceding pages have, I hope, shewn how pecular in every respect are the usages and feelings of the irregular horsemen of India, and the system to be pursued in their management; and I cannot conclude this portion of my subject without pointing out a great improvement which may be made, affecting the regiments of Irregular Cavalry of Hindoostan. Serving as they are in various cantonments and divisions of the army, their commandants being vested with very limited authority, and liable to receive contradictory orders from the different officers under whose command they are placed, which interfere much with the well-being and efficiency of their regiments,—it is almost impossible to continue one uniform system of discipline and internal economy.

The officer commanding the A division (being ignorant, as all officers who have not served with Local Horse must be, of their peculiar customs) may direct the introduction of such and such alterations, in a corps of this description whilst under his orders, which the general commanding the next division the regiment may serve in, might entirely disapprove of, and direct to be cancelled. The Irregular Cavalry are thus subject to a continued series of interferences on the part of officers unacquainted with their formation and their peculiarities, which, to say the least of them, must be injurious and vexatious. To remedy this evil, and, as the corps of Irregular Cavalry in Hindoostan are now so numerous, they might, with advantage, be formed into a separate division of themselves, to be called the "Irregular Cavalry division of the Bengal Presidency," over the whole of which a Brigadier should be appointed for purposes of general control. An officer of high rank and experience in this arm, (and there are many such now in

Hindoostan) should be selected for this situation, vested with the same sort of general control, as the Brigadier commanding the artillery has over all portions of his arm, wherever serving. His should be a kind of roving commission; somewhat like the Inspector-General of Cavalry, and it should be his duty to inspect and report annually upon all the corps of the Irregular Horse. An arrangement of this nature would ensure an uniform system of management in all corps of Irregular Horse, and add greatly to their efficiency.

CHAPTER VII.

Suggestions regarding the introduction of the Sillida-
ree system into Regular Cavalry Regiments, its
supposed advantages, &c. &c.

In submitting the suggestions which this con-
cluding chapter contains, I must admit, that I can
claim no credit on the score of originality. They
were first brought under the consideration of Lord
William Bentinck by an Officer of high rank and
admitted talent; and it was generally believed,
that the proposal was approved of by his Lordship.
But with the usual fate of all Eastern measures for
improvement, it was supposed, that the interest of
a small body,—the loss of off-reckonings to some
half a dozen Colonels, and of the troop contracts
to some few Captains, was looked upon as a matter
of more consequence, than the advantages of the
many and of the state. The scheme, as it was,
I believe, originally submitted, went so far as to

o

propose, that, half of the Regular Cavalry regiments of each Presidency should be transformed into Sillidaree Horse. As the measure is a new and untried one, it would perhaps be preferable to commence the trial upon a smaller scale,—say, with three of the Bengal, two Madras, and one Bombay regiment. It is not proposed to alter the conformation of any of these regiments, as they at present exist, as far as their complement of European and Native officers and their general system of discipline is concerned. It is not intended that they should be made Irregulars. Let not any of my brethren of the Grey Jacket incontinently 'flare up,' nor with an extra touch of '*savageness*' twirl their moustache as their eyes may light on this page. All I ask is " Hear for my cause, and be silent that you may hear." The plan I propose leaves your regiments as they are, except in the matter of ownership of horses, and some difference in pay and dress. By its adoption your service will be rendered a much more popular one ; you will procure a better description of recruits; you and your men will have considerably less trouble, and yet you may be as well mounted as you now are; and may retain, if you are particularly wedded to it, your present system in all essentials.

It appears from returns that were furnished a short time previous to the first agitation of the scheme now mentioned, that the cost to Government of Native Cavalry in different parts of India, was, from 75 Rs. on the Madras to nearly 73 Rs. on the Bombay, and Rs. 54 on the Bengal Presidency.

In Bengal this charge is exclusive of stabling, and every where it is exclusive of the cost of arms, places of arms, camp equipage, and commissariat. There would, therefore, plainly be a saving to Government, if the Sillidaree plan, as follows, were introduced :

First. The proposals are, that, in those corps where the experiment is to be tried, the horses should be transferred from the Government, and made over to the men as their own property; the

latter receiving 40 Co.'s rupees per month for each
man and horse, of which fifteen are to be
considered as the personal pay of the trooper,
and the remaining twenty-five the pay for the
horse.   For the former sum the rider should
furnish every thing, arms, clothing, &c. except
ammunition ; and for the latter, the owner of the
horse should undertake the same contract as the
khooduspa in the Irregular Cavalry which I have
previously explained.

Secondly.   That the present distasteful and un-
becoming uniform should be replaced by another,
more adapted to their tastes and habits,—in short,
by a native for a European costume; and one,
which, the pay of the private (15 rupees) would
enable him to furnish.   As a part of these latter
arrangement, native saddles, or kogheers, and
native sabres should be substituted for those now
in use.

The horses, which are now the property of
Government, might be valued by committees,
and the price deducted from the new Sillidars by

easy instalments. This seems the simplest plan for the first transfer. For the future, as remounts may be required, the Sillidars might easily procure them themselves, or if Government could afford to furnish colts from their studs for the sum of from 400 to 425 rupees these might also be brought before regimental committees, and sold for the price decided on, to the Sillidar. As the pay would be handsome, horses, in every respect as good as those now in the regular regiments of Cavalry, should be insisted on.

The system of keeping a tattoo and a saees for every two horses ought also to be introduced, and those (to the native) most irksome and distasteful of all duties, "stable duties," might be abolished. Native officers, according to their rank, should be permitted to own a certain number of assamees, and a number of subordinary arrangements made, into the details of which, it is needless here to enter. My object is merely to give a rough outline of a plan which has been thought, and which I believe, to possess many and great

advantages; and which might be introduced
with a saving to the State.

The principal advantages are. 1st, that without
affecting the present conformation of these corps,
or their discipline materially, (except as regards
the grooming of their horses) a system is introduced suitable to the tastes and the predilections
of the better and warlike 'classes of India, whom
it should be the object of Government to enlist
in our service. 2ndly, A very superior description of recruit would soon be found *entreating* for
service. 3rdly, The horses, as being their own
property, would be much more carefully looked
after, by the trooper; a weapon that he could
use, and a dress of which would be found, and
in which he would be at ease, are substituted
for arms which in his hands are nearly useless, and a costume of which the trooper is half
ashamed, and which in his heart he loathes.*

---

* In Blackwood, for February, 1845, the following passage occurs
in a review of a work by Major and Mrs. Griffiths, entitled " A
" Journey across the Desert from Ceylon to Marseilles." " When

Lastly, these regiments would not be nearly so costly.

We have the authority of Sir John Malcolm for saying, that " the progress of our power has " been favorable to the commercial community, " and to some of the poorest and most defenceless " of our subjects—but it has been the reverse " to the higher orders of the natives, and to the " military classes. On the remedying of these " defects, the duration of our dominion will, in " a great degree, depend: "—And also, " that the " most important of the lessons we can derive from " past experience is, to be slow and cautious in " every procedure which has a tendency to colli- " sion with the habits and prejudices of our native " subjects. We may be compelled by the character " of our Government to frame some institutions " different from those we found established, but

" Sultan Mahmood stripped off the turban and turned the noble " dress of his people into the caricature of the European costume, " he struck a heavier blow at his sovereignty than ever was " inflicted by the Russian sabre or the Greek dagger. *He smote* " *the spirit of his nation.*"

" we should adopt all we can of the latter into our
" system."

The same high authority lays it down as an
axiom, that the true value of all institutions
depends upon their being in unison with the community and government to which they belong.   If
we desire their stability we must adapt them to
the strength, the weakness, the prejudices, the
virtues, the vices, all the qualities, in short, of
those human beings for whose benefit they are
founded.

The present system which obtains in our regiments of Regular Cavalry is certainly as opposed
to all " the habits and prejudices of our native
subjects " as can well be imagined, whereas the one
now submitted is in unison with their tastes, and
in accordance with the usages with which they
are most familiar, and to which they are most
attached.

It has been the great fault of our Government
that fixed in " the belief of our own superiority,
" we, too often expect and enforce a sudden

" conformity to a system of rule that is opposed to
" every existing feeling and prejudice of the party
" from whom it is exacted."*   We seem to have
taken for granted, that because the European soldier
was good and the system pursued towards him was
found to answer well, that *therefore* the same cause
must necessarily produce the same results in the
native soldier—that what was ' sauce for goose '
must of necessity be also ' sauce for gander.'
Never was policy more short-sighted :—but it is
not yet too late to remedy the errors of the past.
All the immense mass of evidence which has of
late been collected regarding our native army, goes
to prove, that there is a great deterioration since
the ' olden times ' of Clive and Lake.   The
abolishment of the lash, the reduction of pay and
authority in their European officers, and various
other reasons have been assigned as the cause of
this ; but it has always appeared to me as passing

* Minutes, 30th November 1830, Sir J. Malcolm.

P

strange, that with so many officers intimately
acquainted with natives and their feelings, none
should have suggested that our harsh and irksome
system of discipline and drill, so unsuited, so heart-
breaking to the Asiatic, might have materially
assisted towards bringing about the melancholy
result which all confess, and all deplore. Even
now let the trial be made of retaining in our
system all that is not radically bad in the one we
propose to supercede, merely engrafting upon it
such plain and evident improvements, as will tend
to the mutual advantage of the Government and
the governed, and *dovetail*, as it were, with the
usages of the community whose services we wish
to avail ourselves of. I do most firmly believe,
that by such a course of proceeding not only a
more efficient and highly superior description of
Cavalry for all Indian service would be obtained,
but that a great political object might be secured
by affording employment to natives of a higher
rank than those who enter our regular service,

" Who, instead of being the most efficient of all
" ranks to preserve order and give dignity to the
" society to which they belong, and strength to
" the Government to which they owe allegiance,
" are depressed by our levelling system into a
" useless and discontented class. Many, judging
" from results, ascribe to the want of virtue and
" good feeling and to rooted discontent in this
" class, what appears to me to be distinctly attri-
" butable to our own conduct as rulers."*

This proposal has besides this additional value,
that it converts a portion of those who are most
prompt and able to disturb the public peace into
its defenders.

Great opportunities for advancement have been
afforded to the better description of natives in all
civil situations, why close the door to the higher
families of the military class? The operation of
the system that I have ventured to recommend

* Minutes by Sir J. Malcolm, 30th November 1830.

will, not immediately, but in process of time. If
usually preserved in, render situations in corps
thus rendered an object of request to all the
higher and more influential classes, upon whose
condition the same and support demain
pursued serves " the preservation of this empire
has depend."

Printed in the United States
150926LV00004B/13/A